Published by Firefly Books Ltd. 2025

First printing

Library of Congress Control Number: 2024952831

Library and Archives Canada Cataloguing in Publication
Title: Birds life size : up close and personal with 47 bird species / Chris Earley.
Names: Earley, Chris, 1968- author
Description: Includes index.
Identifiers: Canadiana 20250113651 | ISBN 9780228104872 (hardcover)
Subjects: LCSH: Birds—Juvenile literature. | LCSH: Birds—Pictorial works Juvenile literature.
Classification: LCC QL676.2 .E27 2025 | DDC j598—dc23

Published in the United States by
Firefly Books (U.S.) Inc.
P.O. Box 1338, Ellicott Station
Buffalo, New York 14205

Published in Canada by
Firefly Books Ltd.
50 Staples Avenue, Unit 1
Richmond Hill, Ontario L4B 0A7

Cover and interior design: Hartley Millson

Cover photo credits:
Bald Eagle: Shutterstock/Ludo KOOS.
Northern Cardinal: Shutterstock/Bonnie Taylor Barry.
Elf Owl: Shutterstock/AZ Outdoor Photography.
Calliope Hummingbird: Shutterstock/Richard Seeley.
Red-breasted Nuthatch: Shutterstock/Aaron J Hill.
Blue Jay: Shutterstock/FotoRequest.

Printed in China | E

We gratefully acknowledge the financial support of the Government of Canada for our publishing program.

Contents

Introduction

Everyone always asks me what my favorite bird is. You'd think that after watching birds most of my life I would have an answer ready, but I don't. How can I choose? The colors on a Wood Duck, the speed of a Peregrine Falcon, the cuteness of a Black-capped Chickadee ... Every bird species is special in its own way.

This book is a life-sized introduction to 47 bird species. It covers their biology and unique life histories. Immerse yourself in their world as you observe the details of their feathers, wings, beaks, eyes and more. Learn about their interesting behaviors, and see photos that show how they eat, nest and interact. The birds in these pages spend at least some of their lives in North America, but remember that "our" birds may migrate (or travel) and become someone else's birds at certain times of the year.

Hopefully this book will lead you to find out more about these feathered friends — like a particular species' nesting habits, how it finds its food or how far it migrates. I hope these pages also help connect you to birds. Their intelligence, plumage (feathers), flying skills and diversity have captured my heart, and I'm sure they will capture yours as well.

Keys to the Bird Profiles

The bird profiles in this book are grouped by their families (turn to pages 40–41 to learn more about how birds and other animals are classified). Each profile gives you basic bits of information to learn more about that bird species.

Each profile starts with the common name of the species. Underneath the name you can find what family it belongs to.

Each profile features a life-size photo of the bird, and the bird's average body length is given in inches and centimeters. Learn more about measuring birds on pages 22–23.

"Nature Notes," which appear in yellow boxes and circles, give you extra facts about each bird.

This informational box tells you some important things about each bird species, like its scientific name, its habitat (where it lives), its diet (what it eats), its nest site (where it lays its eggs), how far it migrates in the winter and where, generally, it can be found in North America.

When it comes to migration, birds may stay close to their nesting grounds in the winter or fly south, either short or long distances. "Resident" means that birds stay in the same place year-round and can find adequate food sources even during the colder months. "Short distance" means birds may fly up to a few hundred miles, which they often do when they cannot find enough food in the winter. "Long distance" means birds may fly thousands of miles south for the winter. They leave their summer breeding grounds in the northern parts of North America for warmer climates in Central and South America. Some birds may decide to stay put or migrate, depending on how much food is available. These birds may be listed as resident, short distance *and* long distance.

The bird's location gives you a general sense of where in North America it can be found. "NW" stands for northwest, "NE" stands for northeast, "SW" stands for southwest and "SE" stands for southeast. If you're curious about whether a bird appears in your area, try to find its range map online and see if it overlaps with your location.

Canada Goose

Ducks, Geese and Swans

Big and Small

The Canada Goose is found throughout most of North America. Unlike the Red-tailed Hawk (see pages 60–61), it doesn't vary much in color across the continent, but it did once have its own claim to fame when it comes to variation: It had the bird world's widest size range within a single species. This range went from the "Giant" Canada Goose subspecies, which can be more than 45 inches (115 cm) long and weigh over 13¼ pounds (6 kg), down to the 24½-inch (62 cm), 2½-pound (1.1 kg) "Minima Cackling" subspecies. What does that mean? It would be like comparing a goose the size of a Wild Turkey to one the size of a Mallard (see pages 12–13)! This size range made the Canada Goose both the smallest and the largest goose species in the world. In 2004 scientists determined that the four smallest Canada Goose subspecies are different enough from the others to make them their own species. So now there are two species instead of one: the small Cackling Goose *(Branta hutchinsii)* and the large Canada Goose. If Cackling Geese live in your area, try looking closely at the next big flock of Canada Geese you come across and see if you can find some tiny Cackling Geese among them.

Life Size
35½ to 45¼ inches (90–115 cm)

Canada Geese are very protective parents to their small yellow goslings.

Canada Geese in their V flight formation. They are one of the first birds in flight that we learn to identify.

Scientific name: *Branta canadensis*
Habitat: Marshes, lakes and open grassy areas
Diet: Grasses, seeds, grains and berries
Nest site: On the ground, often beside water
Migration: Resident and short distance (though Arctic breeders may spend their winters in the southern United States)
Location: NW NE SW SE

Nature Note

Canada Geese have benefited from the lawn habitats that we have created, which make these birds common in urban areas.

Look at the huge difference in size between this Canada Goose (left) and this Cackling Goose (right).

Trumpeter Swan

Ducks, Geese and Swans

Big Foot of the Bird World

At over 26 pounds (11.8 kg), the massive Trumpeter Swan is North America's heaviest flying bird. From beak tip to tail tip, large males can be almost 6 feet (1.8 m) long. To get something this big into the air requires a lot of propulsion (which is the force that moves things forward or up). The Trumpeter Swan has huge webbed feet that it uses to run along the surface of the water to gather enough speed to take off. Its feet are up to 7 inches (17.8 cm) wide and 7 inches (17.8 cm) long — its footprint would cover a lot of this page you're reading (see the outline behind this text)! As well as making great swimming paddles while on the water, the Trumpeter Swan's large feet are very useful in another way: incubating eggs (which means keeping them warm until they hatch). Mute Swans and many other species of waterfowl pluck feathers from their bellies to create what's called a brood patch. This allows the skin of the bird's belly to be right against its eggs to warm them. Instead of a brood patch, Trumpeter Swans use their large feet to help incubate their eggs. The female's two feet are wide enough to cover her normal clutch of four to six eggs.

Trumpeter Swan tracks

Scientific name: *Cygnus buccinator*
Habitat: Wetlands
Diet: Plants and grains
Nest site: On the shoreline of wetlands
Migration: Resident and short distance
Location: NW NE SW SE

Nature Note

This Trumpeter Swan mom has had all seven of her eggs hatch! Baby swans are called cygnets.

The Trumpeter Swan's big feet are great for sliding along the water's surface during landing.

Wood Duck

Ducks, Geese and Swans

Colorful, Compact and Crafty

The male Wood Duck is one of the most colorful ducks in the world. This waterfowl species is also one of the planet's smallest ducks. Female Wood Ducks weigh just over 1 pound (453 g). They are small enough to fit into small holes in trees and old woodpecker nesting cavities, such as those made by the Pileated Woodpecker (see pages 70–71). She uses these types of cavities as a nesting site, lining it with her own down feathers to help keep her eggs warm. But not all the eggs in her nest are necessarily her own. Wood Ducks and a few other duck species are known as "egg dumpers." This means that some female ducks will lay their eggs in the nests of other females, sometimes even laying them in the nest of another duck species. They then leave those eggs to be raised by the female, who incubates them. Egg dumping is a lot like the old saying "don't put all of your eggs in one basket." If, for example, all your eggs are in one nest and a raccoon finds it, none of your eggs will survive. But if you spread your eggs out, at least some might escape predators and hatch. Birds have evolved many different strategies to make sure that at least some of their young have a chance to become adults and have young of their own.

Once they hatch, Wood Duck ducklings may have to jump from a height of over 50 feet (15.2 m) to join their mother on the ground before they waddle off to the closest pond. That's more than a four-story drop!

In this Wood Duck nest, two Wood Duck eggs and one Hooded Merganser egg have hatched. This shows that a female Hooded Merganser laid at least one egg in this nest. The female Wood Duck incubated it along with her own eggs.

Nature Note

You may be surprised to learn that one of the Wood Duck's favorite foods is acorns! These ducks can sometimes be seen walking along a forest floor looking under oak trees for a snack.

Scientific name: *Aix sponsa*
Habitat: Wetlands and forests
Diet: Seeds, fruits, insects and other invertebrates
Nest site: In holes in trees
Migration: Resident and short distance
Location: NW NE SW SE

Life Size
18½ inches (47 cm)

Mallard

Ducks, Geese and Swans

A Whale of a Bird

If I told you that a Mallard was like a Blue Whale, would you believe me? Well, it's true — at least when it comes to one of the ways they eat. Baleen whales, such as Blue, Minke, Humpback, Gray and Fin whales, feed by scooping large amounts of water filled with fish, krill (small shrimp-like animals) or both into their mouth and then filtering out the food by squeezing the water out of its mouth through special structures called baleen. Mallards, as well as Northern Shovelers, Northern Pintails, Gadwalls and other dabbling ducks (shallow-water ducks that feed near the surface), do the same thing. But instead of having baleen, they have small comb-like structures called lamellae on the sides of their beaks. Have you ever watched a Mallard in a park snapping its beak rapidly at the surface of a muddy puddle or pond? It is filter feeding just like a whale!

This male (left) and female (right) Mallard are filter feeding in a puddle.

The Northern Shoveler is one of the Mallard's close relatives. It is very good at filter feeding because it has a large, wide beak and its lamellae are very close together. This allows this duck species to eat many different sizes of aquatic organisms, including micro-organisms (tiny organisms you need a microscope to see). Look closely to spot the lamellae along the sides of this female Northern Shoveler's beak.

Nature Note

The Mallard is the most common duck in North America. It can be found in many places, including downtown areas of large cities.

Life Size
23 inches (58.4 cm)

Scientific name: *Anas platyrhynchos*
Habitat: Wetlands
Diet: Aquatic invertebrates and seeds
Nest site: On the ground
Migration: Resident and short distance
Location: NW NE SW SE

Mourning Dove

Pigeons and Doves

Quantity over Quality

A Mourning Dove nest is often just a shallow layer of sticks on a ledge or branch — not much of a nursery to hold two gleaming white eggs. You might think this is a terrible way to start a family, but being a careless-but-speedy nest builder is just one of the Mourning Dove's strategies for producing lots of young each year. If the eggs don't fall out of the nest first, the chicks that hatch grow quickly, which means the breeding pair can also start their next brood quickly. The female may even lay her next clutch of eggs in the same nest as the young birds she is currently raising! The Mourning Dove's rapid nesting cycle allows it to have many different broods within the same breeding season: While most small birds have only one or two nesting attempts per year, Mourning Doves can have up to seven!

Scientific name: *Zenaida macroura*
Habitat: Forest edges, shrubby areas, farmland and suburbs
Diet: Seeds
Nest site: On tree branches, shrubs, building ledges and sometimes the ground
Migration: Resident and short distance
Location: NW NE SW SE

This Mourning Dove has built its nest on top of a spiny cactus, which helps protect it.

Mourning Doves almost always lay two eggs.

Nature Note

Like other pigeons and doves, but unlike most other birds, Mourning Doves feed their young something called crop milk. It is a lumpy liquid created in the crop, a part of the bird's esophagus that often stores food. Crop milk is high in protein and fat, which makes it a nutritious meal for growing chicks.

Life Size
12 inches
(30.5 cm)

Greater Roadrunner

Cuckoos

Speed Demon

There are many nifty things about the Greater Roadrunner, but its favorite way of getting around makes it really stand out. While most small birds usually fly to get from point A to point B, the Greater Roadrunner prefers to run. Although it can fly, it spends much of its time doing short running dashes then stopping and looking around for prey. Once it finds a tasty lizard, scorpion or spider, it sprints forward and grabs it with its beak. To kill its meal before swallowing it, the Greater Roadrunner bashes it repeatedly on a rock or on the ground. Greater Roadrunners are capable predators that can also take on larger prey such as rodents, small birds and even rattlesnakes up to 23½ inches (60 cm) long — that's longer than the roadrunner itself!

Life Size
21¼ inches (54 cm)

Nature Note

The Greater Roadrunner can run over 18 miles per hour (29 km/h) for long distances. It uses its long tail to stay balanced when turning at high speeds.

This Greater Roadrunner has caught a large lizard at the edge of a parking lot.

A Greater Roadrunner approaches a rattlesnake. Roadrunners prey on small rattlesnakes, and they also attack larger ones if they get too close to their nests.

Scientific name: *Geococcyx californianus*
Habitat: Dry, shrubby areas and deserts
Diet: Insects, spiders, scorpions, snakes, lizards, rodents, small birds, fruit and seeds
Nest site: On thorny bushes or cacti
Migration: Resident
Location: SW

A Greater Roadrunner running on a road. They often hunt along roadways, where it is easy for them to spot prey.

Common Poorwill

Nightjars

Smallest Beak but Biggest Mouth

When the Common Poorwill is quietly sitting on the ground during the day, its beak is barely visible. But when it takes off at night and finds a flying insect, it opens that tiny beak to reveal a truly cavernous mouth. Having a wide gape (or open mouth) makes catching flying moths and beetles in the dark much easier. All members of the nightjar family (which includes nighthawks and whip-poor-wills) are aerial insectivores (they eat insects while flying) and have big mouths. Birds in this group are also known as "goatsuckers" because shepherds wrongly thought the birds used their large mouths to drink milk from goats at night.

Can you see how tiny the Common Poorwill's beak is when its mouth is shut?

Life Size
7½ to 8¼ inches (19–21 cm)

During the day, sleeping Common Poorwills use their incredible camouflage to stay safe and hidden while roosting on the ground.

Nature Note

Common Poorwills are the only birds in the world that go into a deep hibernation-like state for long periods in the winter — sometimes for almost a month. During this period of inactivity, their body temperature may go down to 41°F (5°C). That's the lowest for any bird! In comparison, yours is usually a constant 98.6°F (37°C).

Scientific name: *Phalaenoptilus nuttallii*
Habitat: Dry, shrubby areas
Diet: Insects
Nest site: On the ground
Migration: Short distance and long distance
Location: NW SW

The Common Poorwill also uses its large mouth to drink while on the fly.

Calliope Hummingbird

Hummingbirds

The Half-Pint Hummer

The Calliope Hummingbird is North America's smallest bird, and it's also one of the smallest birds in the world. It weighs about the same as three paper clips. The eggs of this half-pint hummer, which lives in the mountains of the western United States and Canada, are also very small, measuring just over ¼ by ½ inch (8 by 12 mm) — about the same size as a small blueberry. It lays two eggs in a nest that is equally tiny: only 1½ inches (4 cm) wide and 1¼ inches (3 cm) deep. It builds its nest on a horizontal branch and camouflages it with lichens. Calliope Hummingbirds breed as far north as central British Columbia and spend their winters in southern Mexico. They make this up-to-5,600-mile (9,000 km) round-trip every year. This makes them the smallest long-distance migrant in the bird world.

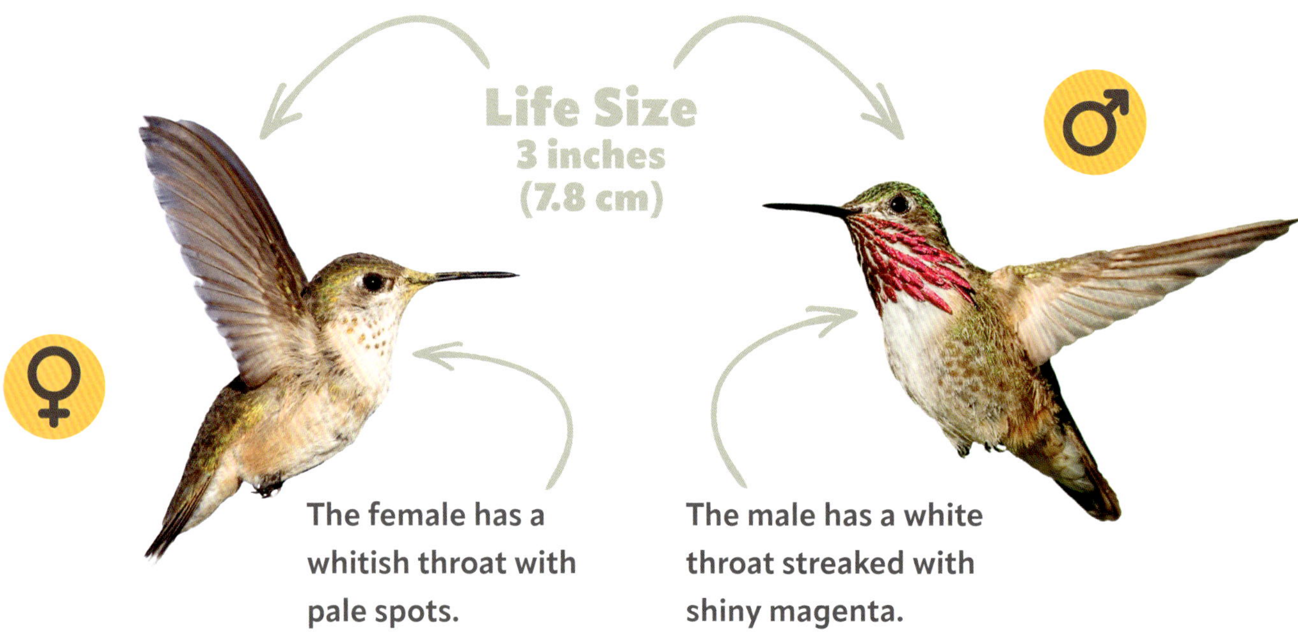

The female has a whitish throat with pale spots.

The male has a white throat streaked with shiny magenta.

A high-energy bird like the Calliope Hummingbird needs high-energy foods, such as flower nectar.

Scientific name: *Selasphorus calliope*
Habitat: Mountains
Diet: Nectar and insects
Nest site: On tree branches
Migration: Long distance
Location: NW SW

Nature Note

Like other North American hummingbirds, female Calliope Hummingbirds build their nests and raise their young with no help from the males.

Measuring Birds

Ornithologists (bird scientists) often need to catch birds and measure them for their research. These measurements can help the researchers learn a lot about our feathered friends. For example, did you know that while the males of many bird species are bigger than the females, in almost all raptors, including hawks, owls and falcons, the females are larger? One theory to explain this is that larger females may be better at protecting the nest from predators. Another interesting fact related to bird size is that individuals in the northern parts of a species range are often larger than those in the southern parts. Being bigger

A pair of Great Horned Owls. The larger female is on the left.

A finch perches on a Prickly Pear Cactus in the Galápagos Islands.

helps them stay warm, which is more of a problem in the northern part of North America than in the south.

Measuring a specific part of a bird can also be very interesting. In the Galápagos Islands, seed sizes and hardness change as the environment changes. Ornithologists have seen that, through many generations, the size of finches' beaks change to the best shape for eating these seeds.

The life-sized photos in this book were a challenge to get just right. To measure a bird's length, scientists gently place it on its back and tilt its head backward to measure from the tip of the beak to the tip of the tail. But most birds are never in this position naturally! Plus, the visible length of a bird depends on its position: Think about the curved neck of a heron or the different postures of a small bird while it's perched. To get the sizing of the birds in this book as true to life as possible, we used beak measurements (which do not change with the bird's position) and compared the birds directly to study skins (stuffed birds) in a wildlife museum.

Depending on how it holds its neck, a Green Heron can really change its size. Compare this Green Heron with the one on the left.

American Coot

Rails

The Coolest Toes

The first time you see an American Coot, you may think you are a looking at some kind of duck — that is, until it gets out of the water and reveals its toes. Ducks, swans and many other waterbirds have webbed feet. This means their toes are connected, which helps them swim on or below the surface of the water. Instead of having webbing between their toes, American Coots have fleshy lobes that grow out the sides of their toes. While odd looking, these round, flat parts still work well for swimming and even diving. They also allow the bird to walk across floating plants without sinking. American Coots make a floating nest that is attached to rooted water plants so it doesn't float away. They usually lay 6 to 12 eggs, and the young often leave the nest when they are just one day old. Although the adults look duck-like, the young coots' curly feathers and red-and-blue heads make them look very different from ducklings.

Unlike ducklings, American Coot chicks have bald heads and curly feathers.

American Coots also use their strange feet for fighting, especially when defending territories.

Scientific name: *Fulica americana*
Habitat: Wetlands
Diet: Plants and seeds
Nest site: Floating nest attached to plants
Migration: Resident, short distance and long distance
Location: NW NE SW SE

Life Size
15 inches (38 cm)

Nature Note

Although they live in similar habitats and have similar shapes, ducks and coots are actually very different. Ducks are more closely related to geese and swans, while coots are closer to cranes and rails.

American Coot toes are lobed on the sides and look quite different from the webbed toes of a duck or a goose.

Killdeer

Plovers

Acting at Its Finest!

Life Size
10 inches
(25 cm)

Killdeers usually lay four eggs. By keeping the narrow end of each egg pointing toward the middle of the clutch, there is less chance of one of them rolling out of the nest.

Killdeer chicks look like fluffy cotton balls on long, spindly legs.

Scientific name: *Charadrius vociferus*
Habitat: Grasslands and open ground
Diet: Insects
Nest site: On the ground
Migration: Resident and short distance
Location: NW NE SW SE

Nesting in the open and on the ground is a risky family plan for a bird. Every animal that eats eggs is a threat. Killdeers increase their odds of success by laying eggs that are well camouflaged (meaning they're hidden) in their rocky nesting sites. But if the worst happens and a predator starts getting close to its nest, the Killdeer has another trick up its sleeve: the broken-wing act. The Killdeer pretends it can't fly and even drags one of its wings along the ground. It also spreads its tail to show a flashy orange patch to attract the predator's attention. Once the predator starts to follow the "injured" bird, the Killdeer walks farther and farther from its nest while still dragging and flapping its wing. Once it has lured the predator a safe distance from the nest, the Killdeer flies away, saving its eggs!

Nature Note

The Killdeer gets its name from its call: *Killdeer! Killdeer! Killdeer!* Onomatopoeia is when something is named for the sound it makes. Other birds with onomatopoeic names in this book include the chickadee and the poorwill.

It may look hurt, but this feathered faker is trying to get a predator to follow it away from its nest to save its eggs.

American Woodcock

Sandpipers and Allies

I'm Peeking, so No Sneaking!

Scientific name: *Scolopax minor*
Habitat: Forests
Diet: Worms and other invertebrates
Nest site: On the ground
Migration: Short distance
Location: NE SE

Life Size
9¾ to 12¼ inches
(25–31 cm)

If you look straight ahead and raise your arms away from your sides, you should be able to *just* see your arms at the edges of your field of vision. This means that you can see about 180 degrees, or halfway around your head, without moving your neck or eyes. Now, imagine if you could see *all* the way around your head (360 degrees) at once. That is how an American Woodcock sees. Its eyes are on the sides and toward the top of its head instead of at the front, like ours. This allows it to always be on the lookout for a predator that may want to sneak up on it. American Woodcocks look for food in wet, shrubby areas with their heads down as their long beaks probe the mud and soil for worms and insects. Having eyes on the sides of their head allows them to be watchful even while feeding.

An American Woodcock sticks its long beak into the soil to find food.

The position of this female American Woodcock's eyes allows her to scan for danger in all directions while she sits on her well-camouflaged nest.

Nature Note

The American Woodcock has earned lots of other names, including Big-eye (for its large eyes), Bogsucker (because it sticks its long beak into wet mud), Labrador Twister (for its twisting flight display) and, everyone's favorite, Timberdoodle (we have no idea why).

Can you see how high the eyes are placed on this American Woodcock's head?

Red Phalarope

Sandpipers and Allies

Flashy Females and Stay-at-Home Dads

If a male and female bird of the same species look different, most of the time it is the male that is the more colorful of the two. As well, if one parent does more work incubating eggs and rearing the young, it is almost always the female. Red Phalaropes don't do either. The female is one of the most colorful shorebirds in the world and is much brighter than the male. Once the female lays her four eggs, she leaves. The male takes over all of the incubation and raises the brood. But he is up for the task. He keeps the eggs warm for about 19 days before they hatch and sometimes does wing-distraction displays (see Killdeer on page 27) to lure away potential nest predators. After the chicks hatch and before they can fly, he will cover them with his body in bad weather and warn them if there are any predators nearby, just like the mom birds of other species. A truly devoted dad!

For 10 to 11 months, Red Phalaropes spend their lives out on the ocean — quite a feat for a bird smaller than an American Robin. This bird is in its non-breeding plumage.

Scientific name: *Phalaropus fulicarius*
Habitat: Tundra (breeding season) and open ocean (non-breeding season)
Diet: Aquatic invertebrates
Nest site: On the ground
Migration: Long distance
Location: NW NE

Nature Note

The other two phalarope species also show "reversed sexual dimorphism," which is a fancy way of saying the females are more brightly colored than the males. The birds above are Red-necked Phalaropes, and the birds below are Wilson's Phalaropes.

Atlantic Puffin

Auks, Murres and Puffins

Mighty Mouth

Known for its colorful beak, the Atlantic Puffin is a seabird of the northeast coast of North America. It swims under ocean waves to catch fish and brings them back to its one chick, which it hides in a burrow not far from the shore. But the puffin has a challenge. It's more efficient for it to bring a bunch of fish to its chick in one trip rather than one at a time. But how can it catch more than one fish after the first one is in its mouth? To do this the puffin uses a cool adaptation: Its tongue and the roof of its mouth have backward-facing spines. This allows the puffin to hold a small, slippery fish across its tongue and the roof of its mouth and still use its beak to catch the next fish. It's so good at this that on average it catches and holds 10 fish at once per trip. However, one hard-working Atlantic Puffin was seen carrying 62 fish at the same time!

Scientific name: *Fratercula arctica*
Habitat: Coasts and open ocean
Diet: Fish
Nest site: In underground burrows
Migration: Resident and short distance
Location: NE

Life Size
12½ inches
(31.8 cm)

An adult Atlantic Puffin peeks out of its burrow.

Not just for fish, a puffin's mouth can also carry nesting material for its burrow.

Nature Note

Natural barriers are one way a bird species may evolve into two or more distinct species. For example, Blue Jays (see pages 80–81) and Steller's Jays likely had a common ancestor that was separated into two groups by the Rocky Mountains. Over many years, the two groups became different species. Oceans can act as natural barriers, too, but not for seabirds, which can cross them relatively easily. That's why Atlantic Puffins are found in both northeastern North America and across the Atlantic in northwestern Europe. However, the land that makes up the North American continent is a barrier for Atlantic Puffins. It separates them from two other puffin species, the Tufted Puffin and the Horned Puffin, both of which are found on the west coast.

Tufted Puffin **Horned Puffin**

Black Skimmer

Gulls and Terns

The Ultimate Underbite

There are a lot of weird beaks in the bird world, but the Black Skimmer's is *really* odd. Its extra-long lower mandible looks like some kind of mistake. However, if a species has survived with a unique adaptation, there is usually a good reason for it. The Black Skimmer's mouth is actually a great hunting tool. A hungry Black Skimmer will fly just above the surface of an ocean or lake with its lower mandible cutting through the water, feeling for fish. As soon as the bird feels something touching its lower mandible, it closes its upper mandible, clamping down on the fish. Since they can grab fish by touch alone, without having to see them, Black Skimmers hunt both at night and during the day.

Scientific name: *Rynchops niger*
Habitat: Wetlands and coasts
Diet: Small fish, sometimes shrimp
Nest site: On the ground
Migration: Resident and short distance
Location: NE SW SE

A Black Skimmer hunts with its lower mandible underwater as it flies.

Nature Note

Some of the Black Skimmer's habitats are very open, which can make it hard to keep their nests safe. That is why the Black Skimmers' eggs are speckled. This patterning helps the eggs blend into their sandy nests.

The Black Skimmer's beak is very thin, which allows it to cut through the water with little resistance.

Common Loon

Loons

Call of the Wild

Common Loons are very vocal waterbirds. They have a variety of different calls, including the wail, the yodel and the hoot. For many species of birds, making and listening to sounds are important for choosing mates, defending territories, finding chicks, warning of danger and staying in a flock. Us humans get to enjoy the beautiful sounds they make when they communicate with each other. Listening to a loon's haunting calls while canoeing a forest-edged lake is a magical experience. However, there is another experience in the Common Loon's habitat that even the birds would agree is less magical: blackflies. Blackflies are tiny biting insects that can be very plentiful in the forested lake areas where Common Loons like to breed. And while these flies are very irritating to humans, they can ruin a Common Loon's nesting success. In some years, there can be so many blackflies that loons sitting on their shoreline nests have to abandon their eggs. Luckily, Common Loons can live for a long time (some have lived to be over 35 years old!), so if they lose a breeding season because of black-flies one year, they will have other chances to raise young in years when blackfly numbers are lower.

Common Loons may abandon their nests when there are too many blackflies.

Nature Note

Can you make a sound like a loon? Find a loon recording online or use the Merlin Bird ID app to listen to their calls and then see if you can imitate them. If you do a good enough job, you can even "talk" to a loon if you visit a place where they breed during the summer!

Scientific name: *Gavia immer*
Habitat: Wetlands
Diet: Fish, crayfish and crabs
Nest site: Just above the shoreline, on the ground
Migration: Short distance and long distance
Location: NW NE SW SE

Anhinga

Darters

The Underwater Spearfisher

Also known as the Water Turkey (for its tail) and Snakebird (for its long neck), the Anhinga is very talented at catching fish. Unlike most other waterbirds, its feathers do not shed water and can get quite wet. The Anhinga also has dense bones, and its bones and wet feathers allow it to sink under the water's surface. It can then slowly move around and sneak up on fish. Once in range of a meal, it quickly thrusts its long, thin neck to spear a fish with its sharp beak. The Anhinga then brings the fish to the surface, throws it into the air and catches it in its mouth. Anhingas always swallow fish head-first. Getting so wet does mean that the Anhinga can lose a lot of body heat when it's swimming. To warm up, it spends some of its day sitting in the sun drying out its feathers.

An Anhinga always swallows fish headfirst, so the spines don't get caught in its throat.

This Anhinga has speared its fishy meal.

This male Anhinga is spreading its wings to help its feathers dry out in the sun.

Nature Note

Being able to stay submerged also helps the Anhinga hide from predators. Anhingas only need to stick their heads above the surface to check for danger, like this one is doing.

Scientific name: *Anhinga anhinga*
Habitat: Wetlands
Diet: Fish, some insects and crustaceans
Nest site: On tree branches above water
Migration: Resident and short distance
Location: SE

Life Size
33 inches
(83.8 cm)

Classifying Birds

Classifying different organisms into groups helps us understand our world. Scientists take similar groups and then divide them into smaller groups. The table below presents the categories we use to show how different organisms are related to each other. Birds all share the same kingdom, phylum and class. Some different animal species are also shown so you can see how they are related to birds. (Note: while only animals are listed below, other groups, such as plants and fungi, are also classified using similar categories.)

	Monarch Butterfly	**Human**	**Mallard**	**Blue Jay**	**Steller's Jay**
Kingdom	Animalia (Animals)	Animalia (Animals)	Animalia (Animals)	Animalia (Animals)	Animalia (Animals)
Phylum	Arthropoda (Arthropods)	Chordata (Chordates)	Chordata (Chordates)	Chordata (Chordates)	Chordata (Chordates)
Class	Insecta (Insects)	Mammalia (Mammals)	Aves (Birds)	Aves (Birds)	Aves (Birds)
Order	Lepidoptera (Butterflies & Moths)	Primates (Primates)	Anseriformes (Screamers, Swans, Geese & Ducks)	Passeriformes (Perching Birds)	Passeriformes (Perching Birds)
Family	Nymphalidae (Brush-footed Butterflies)	Hominidae (Great Apes)	Anatidae (Swans, Geese & Ducks)	Corvidae (Ravens, Crows & Jays)	Corvidae (Ravens, Crows & Jays)
Genus	*Danaus* (Tiger Butterflies)	*Homo* (Humans)	*Anas* (Pintails & Relatives)	*Cyanocitta* (Blue & Steller's Jays)	*Cyanocitta* (Blue & Steller's Jays)
Species	*Danaus plexippus* (Monarch)	*Homo sapiens* (Modern Human)	*Anas platyrhynchos* (Mallard)	*Cyanocitta cristata* (Blue Jay)	*Cyanocitta stelleri* (Steller's Jay)

Some classification goes beyond the species level. For example, Steller's Jays have 16 or 17 subspecies. These are smaller populations in different parts of the jay's range that have slightly different plumages (feathers) and measurements. Can you see the differences in plumage between the two Steller's Jay subspecies shown above?

Knowing how different organisms are related can also help us see how evolution works. For example, hawks and falcons look similar, and both are predators that use their feet to catch their prey. While you may think that this means they are closely related, that is not the case. Recent research has shown that falcons are more closely related to parrots than to hawks. This means that being good flyers and catching prey with their feet have independently evolved in two different groups of birds, resulting in predators that look and act a lot alike but are not closely related.

The Peregrine Falcon (center) is more closely related to the Eclectus Parrot (right) than the Broad-winged Hawk (left).

American White Pelican

Pelicans

The Baggy-Beaked Bird

This majestic bird has a long list of awards. It competes with the California Condor for the widest wingspan of any bird in North America — at over 9 feet (2.7 m). That is about the same as 10 of these books laid end to end on the floor! The American White Pelican also has the longest beak in North America. It measures up to 14 inches (36 cm). And that beak holds the largest volume: About 3 gallons (11.4 L) of water can fit in there. That would be like you holding three large jugs of milk in your mouth. The American White Pelican uses its beak's expandable bag (called a gular pouch) to catch fish. It scoops both fish and water inside its mouth then squeezes the water out. While North America's other pelican, the Brown Pelican, dives from the air and plunges beak first into the water to grab fish, the American White Pelican scoops them up while floating on the water's surface. To be more successful fishers, American White Pelicans often swim together in groups to drive fish into shallow water. They then scoop with their mouths all at the same time so fewer fish can escape.

What a beak! American White Pelicans grow "horns" like this on the top of their beaks during the breeding season. Scientists believe these growths may help the birds attract a mate.

Nature Note

American White Pelicans lay two eggs, but usually only one chick survives.

Feeding together helps herd fish so they are easier to catch.

Scientific Name: *Pelecanus erythrorhynchos*
Habitat: Lakes and oceans
Diet: Fish
Nest site: On the ground
Migration: Short distance and long distance
Location: NW NE SW SE

Life Size
50 inches to 65 inches (127–165 cm)

American Bittern

Herons

Hide-and-Seek Champion

This American Bittern has caught a fishy meal.

The American Bittern is in the heron family and is 28 inches (71 cm) long. You would think it would be hard for this large bird to hide, but not so. American Bitterns often live in marshes. If they feel threatened, they point their beaks to the sky. Their striped undersides help them blend into the vertical lines of the marsh plants camouflaging them. However, their habitat is densely vegetated (meaning it has a lot of plants), so it can be hard for them to find each other during the breeding season. To solve this problem, their call is low pitched and travels far, so they can hear each other across the marsh. The call is an odd gulping noise, often described as a repeated *pump-er-lunk*. This sound has given the American Bittern some fun names, such as "Water Belcher" and "Thunder Pumper."

Scientific name: *Botaurus lentiginosus*
Habitat: Wetlands
Diet: Insects, fish and frogs
Nest site: Just above water in plants
Migration: Short distance and long distance
Location: NW NE SW SE

Nature Note

Unlike many other heron species, female American Bitterns raise their young on their own, without help from the males.

Even out in the open, their amazing camouflage works.

Green Heron

Herons

Fish Beware!

From the giant Great Blue Heron to the tiny Least Bittern, members of the heron family are known for being good fishers. But the small Green Heron takes fishing one step further: It sometimes uses bait. A Green Heron uses food items, such as insects or crusts of bread, and even non-food items, like feathers, twigs or leaves, to attract fish to the surface of the water. Once a fish is within striking distance, the heron quickly extends its long neck and grabs the fish with its big beak. If the bait starts to float away, the fisher will bring it back to a spot within striking distance. This hunting behavior makes Green Herons one of the few bird species in the world that are true tool users.

This Green Heron has laid two bluish eggs. She may lay up to three more.

An alert mother Green Heron and three of her chicks.

A Green Heron carries a piece of bread to use as bait at its favorite fishing spot.

Scientific name: *Butorides virescens*
Habitat: Wetlands
Diet: Fish, amphibians, insects and other invertebrates
Nest site: On the ground or tree branches
Migration: Resident, short distance and long distance
Location: NW NE SW SE

Nature Note

Using tools was once thought to be a human-only trait, but there are many examples of non-human animals using tools, especially in the bird world. In North America, Brown-headed Nuthatches use pieces of bark to pry other pieces of bark off tree trunks as they search for food. American Crows, Common Ravens and Peregrine Falcons all have been recorded dropping rocks on potential predators that come too close to their nests.

Roseate Spoonbill

Spoonbills and Ibises

Why Are There Salad Tongs on Your Face?

Life Size
31 inches (78.7 cm)

The well-named Roseate (meaning "rose-colored") Spoonbill is a favorite bird for anyone visiting Florida and states along the Gulf of Mexico. Its ridiculous beak may seem to be there just to make us smile, but it is a well-adapted hunting tool. The spoonbill feeds by sweeping its beak back and forth in the water as it wades through its wetland habitat. When a small fish or invertebrate touches the spoon part, the bird quickly clamps its beak shut and then swallows its food whole. It hunts mostly by touch, so its bill's wide spoon tip probably increases its chances of catching its prey. The Roseate Spoonbill is still rather rare in the United States. It was once hunted for its beautiful feathers, which were used in hats as decoration. Since hunting it became illegal, the Roseate Spoonbill's numbers have been slowly increasing.

A Roseate Spoonbill sweeps its beak through the water.

Scientific name: *Platalea ajaja*
Habitat: Wetlands
Diet: Fish, crustaceans and insects
Nest site: In trees and shrubs
Migration: Resident and short distance
Location: SE

Nature Note

To see why the spoonbill's beak shape is important, try this experiment:

1. Fill a large bowl with 10 jelly beans.
2. Shut your eyes and try to grab as many jelly beans as you can in one minute using only a pair of chopsticks.
3. Now try the experiment again using salad tongs instead of chopsticks.

Which tool worked better? Which one is more like a spoonbill's beak?

The spoonbill also uses its strangely shaped beak to preen its brilliant feathers.

Turkey Vulture

Vultures

Nature's Clean-up Crew

Death is a natural part of the cycle of life. When animals die or a predator doesn't eat all its prey, nature has a special task force to deal with the leftovers, which are called carrion. One such carcass eater is the Turkey Vulture. Carrion is the main part of its diet, but finding it is a challenge. While the vultures in Africa can see dead animals across the open savanna, much of the Turkey Vulture's range is covered in thick forests. It's nearly impossible for them to see carrion on the ground. The Turkey Vulture overcomes this problem with a special adaptation: its superb nose. Even when it is gliding high above the woods, it can smell rotting flesh so well that it knows in which direction to fly to find it. Finding food by smell is rare in birds that are not open-ocean hunters, such as albatrosses and petrels. This ability has likely helped Turkey Vultures to expand their ranges northward by finding roadkill that is lying along highway edges.

Turkey Vultures spend much of their day flying overhead, smelling for carrion.

Nature Note

Turkey Vultures have strong stomach acid. It kills the harmful bacteria in a rotten carcass so the vulture doesn't get sick.

Life Size
27 inches (69 cm)

Scientific name: *Cathartes aura*
Habitat: Forests, fields and farmland
Diet: Carrion
Nest site: On the floor of a cave or old barn
Migration: Resident, short distance and long distance
Location: SW SE

A young Turkey Vulture peeks out of the barn loft where it hatched.

Bald Eagle

Hawks, Eagles and Allies

A Recovery Success Story

Bald Eagles are now fairly common birds across much of North America, but that wasn't always the case. In 1967 this species was listed as endangered in the United States. Bald Eagle numbers had crashed because of pesticides (which are chemicals used to kill insects that eat crops) like DDT. Eagles were also killed by hunting, trapping and poisoning. Bald Eagle numbers started to increase once DDT was outlawed, hunting was reduced and more habitats were protected. In 2007 the Bald Eagle was removed from the endangered species list, and the population continues to recover in many areas. Bald Eagles are also less scared of people since they're no longer being hunted. Their nesting sites now include areas where humans live, allowing us to watch them hunt and even raise their young right before our eyes.

Here is a parent Bald Eagle with its chick.

Scientific name: *Haliaeetus leucocephalus*
Habitat: Areas with water
Diet: Fish, waterfowl, other medium-sized vertebrates and carrion
Nest site: In trees
Migration: Resident and short distance
Location: NW NE SW SE

With their white heads and tails, adult Bald Eagles are easy to identify.

Nature Note

Nesting platforms have helped increase the number of Bald Eagles.

Life Size
34 inches (86 cm)

Snail Kite

Hawks, Eagles and Allies

Escargot Eater

When it comes to food, some birds are generalists. American Crows, for example, eat a wide variety of foods. Some birds are specialists. These birds eat very few types of foods. Snail Kites are extreme specialists: They eat Apple Snails, a type of freshwater snail, and rarely eat anything else. A Snail Kite has special equipment for eating Apple Snails: Its beak is thin, long and curved. It uses its beak to cut the muscle that attaches the snail to its shell. Once it does this, it can remove the snail's whole body from the shell and eat it. Snail Kites are an endangered species in the United States, meaning there are not many of them left. They occur in Florida, where the massive draining of wetlands in the early 1900s destroyed much of the Snail Kite's and Apple Snail's habitat. This meant fewer Snail Kites could live and raise young there. Wetland management practices are now protecting and even increasing Snail Kite habitat, so hopefully these snail specialists will be around forever.

Scientific name: *Rostrhamus sociabilis*
Habitat: Wetlands
Diet: Apple Snails
Nest site: On the branches of small trees, shrubs and cattails
Migration: Resident and short distance
Location: SE

A male Snail Kite grips the Apple Snail shell with his talons and uses his sharp beak to extract his meal.

This male Snail Kite shows off his specialized snail-extracting beak.

This female Snail Kite carries her snail prey to a feeding perch.

Nature Note

Florida is the extreme northern range of the Snail Kite. They are also found from Mexico to central South America — all places where Apple Snails occur.

Studying Birds

I hope that this book gets you excited about going outside and watching the birds in your neighborhood. The first step is usually to identify the bird. You can then look it up in a book or on the internet to learn more about it. But even if you can't identify the bird you're looking at, you can still observe its behavior. You can do this with any species of bird. Here we will use Rock Pigeons as an example because they are found in many areas, can be quite tame and their color variations make it is easier to know which individual you are watching. Ask yourself these questions:

- How is the pigeon I am looking at interacting with others in the flock? Is it pushy? Is it chasing or being chased by other pigeons?
- How does the pigeon find and pick up food? Does it look at its food directly in front (like we do), or does it turn its head and look at it with one eye? Does it pick up the food quickly, or is it choosy?
- Does the pigeon change its body position or do any strange movements? Is it making these movements near other pigeons? How does it walk? Does it hop?

This male Rock Pigeon (on the left) is chasing a female and displaying for her.

The white markings on this Rock Pigeon will help you find it again if you often visit the same park. Taking a photo or doing a quick sketch (of both sides of the bird) can help you remember exactly what markings to look for.

If you are lucky enough to have a bird feeder, you can watch bird behavior right in your own yard. Ask yourself these questions:

- Are some birds able to push or scare away other bird species from the feeder? Does size affect which birds scare and which birds are scared?
- What seeds do each bird species seem to prefer? Do they eat the seeds at the feeder or carry them away to another spot?
- Which birds arrive in a flock? Which come alone? Do they visit the feeder at specific times of the day?
- What happens when a predator such as a hawk or a cat shows up? Do the birds hide and be quiet, or do they make a lot of noise? Do the birds make any specific sounds when a predator is nearby?

Studying birds is fun and can lead to scientific discovery. Can you make a focused study on what you are seeing? For example, you could search for an unusual-looking pigeon at a city park and study it as an individual every time you visit the park. What size flock is it in? Does it associate with the same pigeons each time or different ones? Is it always in the same spot? When watching a feeder, you could chart out a hierarchy of species from most to least dominant. Is it a direct line, or are some species at the same level? You could also do a seed preference study to figure out what the most important seeds are at your feeder. The possibilities are endless!

A male House Sparrow and a male Downy Woodpecker battle over a suet feeder.

A female Northern Cardinal tries to scare a female Brown-headed Cowbird off the feeder.

Great Horned Owl

Tigers of the Sky

When it comes to being a predator, it is hard to beat the Great Horned Owl. While they often focus on eating small rodents (like mice and rats) and rabbits, these owls have been known to catch and eat skunks, house cats, young foxes, porcupines, turtles, fish, frogs, crayfish and earthworms. There are even records of them killing large birds, such as Red-tailed Hawks and Great Blue Herons. Their talons are long and curved and can squeeze with a lot of power. The amount of force it takes to lift over 28 pounds (13 kg) is the same amount of force it takes to open the gripping foot of a Great Horned Owl. They also use this power to protect their eggs and young, so nest predators beware!

A Great Horned Owl in its nest with three chicks.

The very strong and sharp talons of a Great Horned Owl.

Nature Note

Like most other owls, Great Horned Owls don't make their own nests. If you see one sitting in a nest made of sticks high in a tree, the owl has likely taken it over from a crow or hawk.

Scientific name: *Bubo virginianus*
Habitat: Various, including forests, grasslands, deserts and even suburbs
Diet: Small mammals plus many other animals
Nest site: In holes in trees, on cliff ledges or in trees
Migration: Resident
Location: NW NE SW SE

Life Size
18 to 24¾ inches (46–63 cm)

Snowy Owl

The Arctic Wanderer

Owls

Life Size
23½ inches (60 cm)

Scientific name: *Bubo scandiacus*
Habitat: Tundra and sometimes fields, farmland and coasts
Diet: Rodents, hares, waterfowl, seabirds and other small- to medium-sized vertebrates
Nest site: On the ground
Migration: Resident and short distance
Location: NW NE

The sharp talons of this Snowy Owl help it catch rodents that it can't even see under the snow. Its superb hearing allows it to pinpoint where its prey is hiding.

Everyone remembers seeing their first Snowy Owl, and if you haven't seen one yet, it will certainly be worth the wait! These huge northern raptors are beautiful, tough and adaptable. Their white feathers help them blend into their often-snowy habitats. While they can stay all winter in the Arctic, their survival depends on the amount of food available. If there isn't enough for them to eat, such as during periods when the lemming (a type of small rodent that looks a bit like a hamster) population is low, some Snowy Owls will migrate south to the northern mainland United States and southern Canada. Here they can be found hunting voles and other rodents in open farmland, fields and prairies. Interestingly, the owls may not return to their original territories when they migrate back north, like most other migrant birds do. Snowy Owls will wander to any area that has enough food for them to raise young. They sometimes move east to west and back again. This could result in a Canadian-born Snowy Owl ending up with a nest in the Russian Arctic, for example. They are true explorers!

An adult male Snowy Owl with almost all-white plumage.

Nature Note

Female and young male Snowy Owls often have a lot of dark brown bands on their breast and back feathers. Fully adult male Snowy Owls can be almost all white.

Elf Owl

Owls

Tiny Teamwork

Scientific name: *Micrathene whitneyi*
Habitat: Deserts and dry forests
Diet: Insects, other invertebrates, small lizards and young rodents
Nest site: In holes in trees or cacti
Migration: Resident and short distance
Location: SW

The Elf Owl is the world's smallest owl and is shorter than most sparrows! Elf Owls are tiny and their prey is tiny, too. Favorite foods include moths, crickets and beetles, but they will also eat spiders, scorpions, centipedes, small lizards and young rodents, like mice. Because Elf Owls are so small, they must also make sure that they don't become prey themselves. They protect their eggs and nestlings by nesting in small, abandoned woodpecker cavities (or holes), either in trees or large cacti. Most of the time, a pair of Elf Owls will forcefully defend their territory from other Elf Owls. If, however, there's a potential predator — such as a Great Horned Owl, Gopher Snake or Ringtail — in the area, Elf Owls from neighboring territories may team up to attack the predator and drive it away.

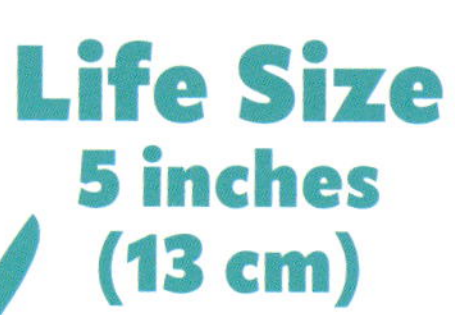

Life Size
5 inches (13 cm)

Nature Note

Some other small owl species, like the Whiskered Screech-Owl and the Western Screech-Owl, live in the Elf Owl's range but do not migrate. The Elf Owl, however, is so tiny that it might not be able to handle colder winter temperatures without its insect prey, so it migrates south for the winter in much of its range.

Camouflage is another important strategy that keeps this little owl safe. Their colors and patterns are the same as their habitat, which makes it more difficult to see them.

A male Elf Owl offers his mate a caterpillar. Yum!

Pileated Woodpecker

Packing a Powerful Punch

The Pileated Woodpecker is North America's largest woodpecker species and an impressive resident of forested areas across the continent. It is a powerful bird. It uses its large, chisel-like beak to chop into trees to get to its favorite food: carpenter ants. The resulting squarish holes with piles of wood chips under them are a sure sign that a Pileated Woodpecker is in the neighborhood. Pileated Woodpeckers also make large, round holes that they use as nesting sites. When the woodpecker is done with its nest, other animals, such as Northern Saw-whet Owls, Wood Ducks, Hooded Mergansers, flying squirrels and tree-climbing snakes, may move in.

These three baby Pileated Woodpeckers are telling their parents they are hungry!

Scientific name: *Dryocopus pileatus*
Habitat: Forests
Diet: Insects, berries and nuts
Nest site: In holes in trees
Migration: Resident
Location: NW NE SE

This Northern Saw-whet Owl has moved into an abandoned Pileated Woodpecker nesting hole.

Both male and female Pileated Woodpeckers have red crests, but the female has a black forehead and mustache. The male, shown here, has a red forehead and mustache.

Nature Note

The Pileated Woodpecker is the largest woodpecker species in North America, but this wasn't always so. The Ivory-billed Woodpecker, found in the southern states, was even bigger than the Pileated Woodpecker. Sadly, it is likely extinct because much of its habitat has been lost because of human activity.

Life Size
17 inches (43 cm)

Peregrine Falcon

Falcons and Caracaras

The Avian Bullet

Look closely and you can spot the tubercle that helps stop air from rushing into the falcon's nostril.

Scientific name: *Falco peregrinus*
Habitat: Open areas
Diet: Birds and bats
Nest site: On cliffs, buildings, branches of tall trees and, in tundra habitats, on the ground
Migration: Resident, short distance and long distance
Location: NW NE SW SE

Life Size
16 inches (40.6 cm)

This Peregrine Falcon is in a stoop. Can you see its raindrop shape?

Peregrine Falcons have long, pointed wings.

Nature Note

Peregrine Falcons eat mostly birds. They can catch everything from a sparrow to a large duck!

The Peregrine Falcon is the fastest animal on Earth. A pilot diving his plane at 175 miles per hour (282 km/h) was passed by a diving Peregrine that was hunting a flock of ducks below. That means the falcon was flying over 100 miles per hour (161 km/h) faster than the speed limit on most interstate highways! To go this fast, Peregrine Falcons need some special adaptations. Their long, pointed wings allow them to fly quickly in flapping flight. During a dive, which is also called a stoop, they tuck in their wings to make their overall body shape like that of a raindrop. This helps them cut through the air with less resistance, which allows them to go faster. One problem they must overcome at such high speeds is air rushing into their nostrils. Peregrine Falcons have a special structure called a tubercle in each nostril. The tubercles slow the air down so the falcon can breathe without air rushing into its body while it is stooping. They also need to protect their eyes. All birds have nictitating membranes, which are clear third eyelids. For Peregrines, this membrane works like a pair of safety goggles that protects their eyes during a dive. These and other adaptations help Peregrines go over 200 miles per hour (322 km/h) to catch their prey of pigeons, ducks, gulls and other birds. Because Peregrine Falcons are now found nesting in cities, where lots of people live, you may have the opportunity to see one hunting, so keep your eyes to the skies!

Great Crested Flycatcher

Tyrant Flycatchers

Life Size
$8\frac{1}{2}$ inches
(21.5 cm)

Tricky Home Decorators

The Great Crested Flycatcher is one of North America's largest flycatchers. It is a common summer breeding bird in eastern forests. Like the Wood Duck and Tree Swallow, the Great Crested Flycatcher uses old woodpecker nesting holes as its nesting sites. But unlike these other bird species, the Great Crested Flycatcher has a special decorating technique when it builds its nest: It sometimes adds the shed skin of a snake! It is thought that the snakeskin may scare away nest predators such as squirrels and mice. They will think there is an actual snake inside. It's sort of like having a "Beware of Dog" sign when you don't have a dog — but a stranger doesn't know that. Isn't that tricky?

Scientific name: *Myiarchus crinitus*
Habitat: Forests
Diet: Insects, other invertebrates and some fruit
Nest site: In holes in trees and in bird boxes
Migration: Long distance
Location: NE SE

This flycatcher's eggs rest in a nest lined with a snakeskin.

A Great Crested Flycatcher has left its hunting perch and is chasing a flying insect.

Nature Note

Because they are so big, Great Crested Flycatchers can catch and eat large insects. Butterflies, dragonflies, grasshoppers and large spiders are all on the menu. They sometimes catch small lizards, and one was even seen eating a Ruby-throated Hummingbird! This individual has caught a swallowtail butterfly.

Helping Birds

Right now, you are already doing one of the best things you can do to help birds — reading this book! When you learn more about different ecosystems and the birds that live in them, you see how important they are. Humans tend to focus on our own wants and needs, but birds and other wildlife deserve their space, too. We have destroyed much of their habitat. We need to take care of the places where our winged neighbors live.

One way you can help directly is by building and installing bird boxes with your family. The number of cavity-nesting birds depends on the number of usable nest cavities. We humans don't value dead trees, so we remove them because we think they look ugly. But when we remove dead and dying trees, we remove places where woodpeckers can create their nest cavities. The birds that use old woodpecker holes for their own nests are also affected. Ask your parents if you can talk to your local naturalist club or search the internet to find building plans for the bird boxes that work best for your area.

Windows can be deadly to birds. They can hit the glass so hard they can die. If your house has a particular window that birds hit, try to find a way to break up the reflection on the outside of the

A female and male Wood Duck check out a large bird box made especially for them!

A male Eastern Bluebird feeds one of his nestlings at a bird box.

glass. Window markers can be very helpful. A more permanent solution is applying stickers that are specifically made to stop birds from hitting windows.

You can also see if your town or city has a program to encourage buildings to shut their lights off at night. Many small birds migrate at night. Thousands hit the windows of tall buildings on their northward or southward migrations. They are attracted to and confused by the lights. You can help by spreading the word. There are also organizations that look for stunned birds in the early mornings and bring them to a wildlife rehabilitation facility. Ask your parents if you can get involved and volunteer.

I put these dots on the outside of my back window, near my feeder. These dots stop the birds from thinking they can fly to the trees they see reflected in the glass. From the inside (see right), the dots blend into the background and don't distract us when we're watching the feeder.

I used a special window marker to draw this Blue Jay design on the outside of another window to stop birds from hitting it.

Blue Jay

Crows, Ravens and Jays

True Blue ... But How?

We love the amazing variety of colors in birds' feathers, and the Blue Jay's blue plumage is a favorite. But where does that blue come from? Birds get their colors in two different ways. One is through pigments that birds get from their food. For example, some plants produce pigments called carotenoids. Birds that eat these plants or eat the insects that eat these plants can produce feathers that could be red like a cardinal, yellow like a goldfinch or orange like an oriole. But other brilliant feathers, like those that appear blue, are not colored using pigments. With these types of feathers, our eyes see certain colors because of how the feather is structured. The microscopic shape of a feather's surface and how it holds air pockets can cause the feather to scatter only blue light to your eye. This is why Blue Jays appear so brilliantly blue. However, if the feathers don't get enough light or are lit from behind, the structures don't scatter light well, and the blue disappears. A red-pigmented feather will look red from all angles. The next time you find a colorful feather, hold it up so that the light is coming from behind it: Does the feather still show its full color?

Scientific name: *Cyanocitta cristata*
Habitat: Forests
Diet: Nuts, seeds, fruits, insects, spiders and small vertebrates
Nest site: On tree branches
Migration: Resident and short distance
Location: NW NE SE

Life Size
11 inches (27.9 cm)

Two Blue Jays argue near a backyard bird feeder.

The Blue Jay's western cousin, the Steller's Jay, also sports some lovely blue feathers.

Nature Note

The red in the above Northern Cardinal's feathers is from pigments. Pigments are used to color things like paint. The blue in this Blue Jay feather (below) is caused by how light hits the structure of the feather. Many other blue things in nature have the same properties. For example, the blue on the surface of a blueberry is also caused by how light hits the structure of the berry's surface.

American Crow

Crows, Ravens and Jays

Lending a Helping Hand ... Er, Beak

A young American Crow waits for a meal from one of its parents ... Or maybe from a helper.

American Crows are one of the most commonly seen birds in North America. We know they are smart, tricky, adaptable and opportunistic, but watching their behavior can be difficult. Crows can be cautious around humans. Luckily, scientists have been studying crows for a long time, and they have made some great observations about the American Crow. For example, did you know that breeding pairs often have help raising their young? Not all crow pairs have helpers but many do, often more than one. These helpers can include young from the previous year's clutch and older birds. Some of these older birds are not even related to the breeding pair. Helpers have been seen bringing sticks to the nest, helping to build the nest, cleaning the nest, feeding the incubating female and the chicks in the nest, and feeding and guarding the young birds after they leave the nest. Both the breeding pair and the helpers likely benefit from this arrangement: The breeding pair gets help with childcare, and young helpers gain experience and learn how to be successful parents when they are older.

An American Crow gives the person watching it a curious look.

This American Crow has scored some French fries.

Scientific name: *Corvus brachyrhynchos*
Habitat: Various, including forests, farmland, coasts and urban areas
Diet: Insects, crabs, fish, reptiles, amphibians, small birds, birds' eggs, small mammals, seeds, nuts, fruit, carrion and garbage
Nest site: On tree branches or shrubs, less commonly on the ground
Migration: Resident and short distance
Location: NW NE SW SE

Nature Note

Many other social animal parents get help with childcare from other members of their group. These include elephants, wolves, chimpanzees and humans!

Life Size
17 inches (43.2 cm)

Black-capped Chickadee

Chickadees

Bird Brainiacs

Scientific name: *Poecile atricapillus*
Habitat: Forests
Diet: Insects, seeds and berries
Nest site: In holes in trees and in bird boxes
Migration: Resident
Location: NW NE SW SE

Black-capped Chickadees are surely one of the cutest birds in the world. Not only do they have big, puffy heads and short, little beaks, but they are also one of the friendliest birds. If you offer them food, they may take it right from your hand! But did you know they also have an excellent memory? In the fall and winter, a chickadee will store hundreds of food items every day and remember where each one is for weeks. Favorite hiding spots include under bark, among dead leaves and even in cracks in the siding of houses. It also remembers if it has already eaten a stored snack and where it hid its favorite food items. These abilities allow chickadees to survive northern winters, when food is scarce and it can be hard to stay warm.

Life Size
4¾ to 5½ inches (12–14 cm)

Nature Note

Black-capped Chickadees are one of North America's most common bird feeder visitors.

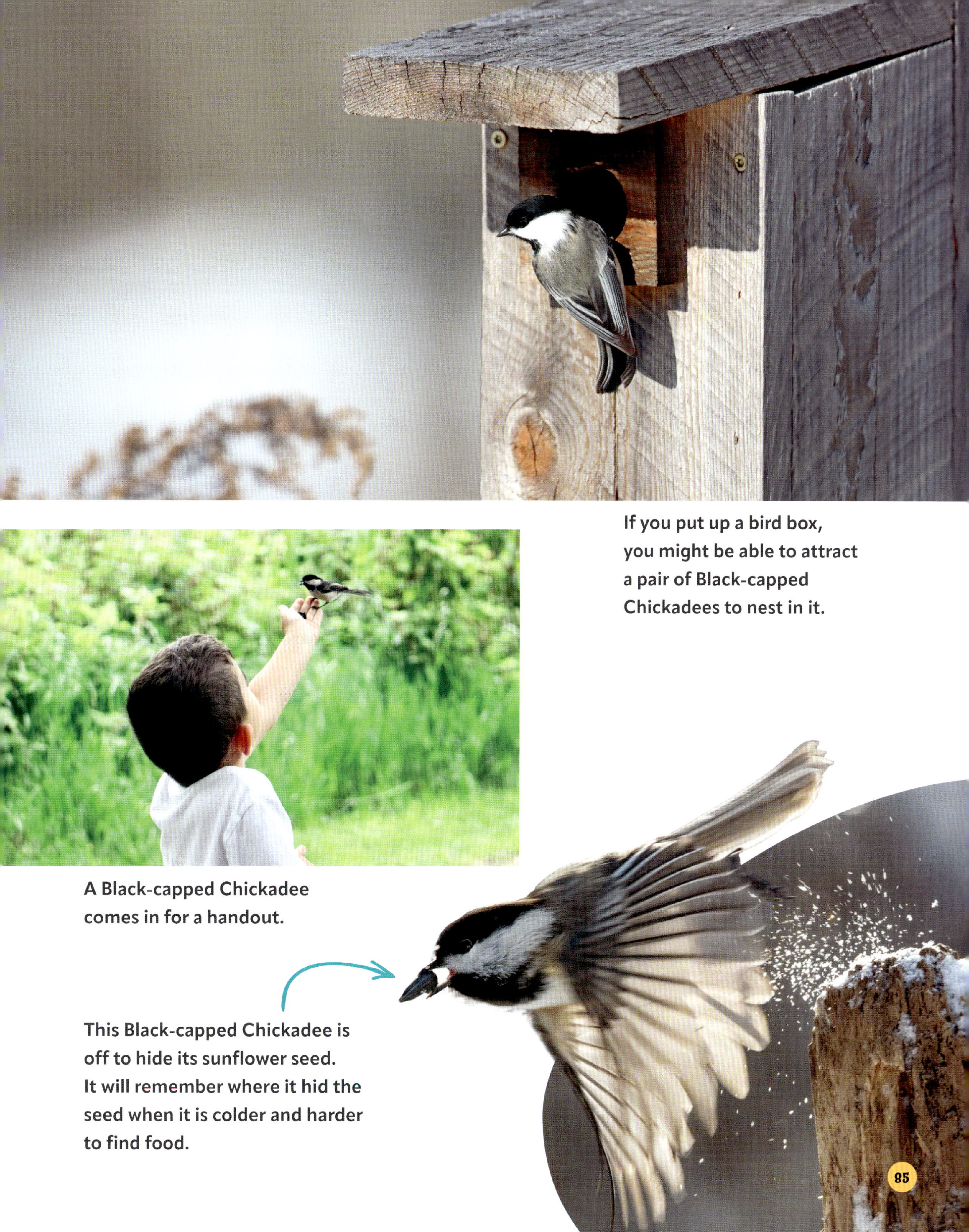

If you put up a bird box, you might be able to attract a pair of Black-capped Chickadees to nest in it.

A Black-capped Chickadee comes in for a handout.

This Black-capped Chickadee is off to hide its sunflower seed. It will remember where it hid the seed when it is colder and harder to find food.

Tree Swallow

Swallows

A Homey Hole for the Best Nest

Tree Swallows nest in, you guessed it, trees. But instead of building a typical bird nest with sticks, they nest in holes in dead trees. Considered a "secondary cavity nester," a Tree Swallow never digs out the hole that it nests in. It usually finds an abandoned tree cavity that was made by a woodpecker (a "primary cavity nester"). Once it finds an appropriate hole, the Tree Swallow lines it with a nest of grasses and feathers. There it lays its eggs and raises its young. Unfortunately, there often aren't enough abandoned woodpecker holes for everyone. They must fight other Tree Swallows and other secondary cavity nesters, such as House Wrens and Eastern Bluebirds, to claim their would-be homes.

Life Size
5½ inches (14 cm)

Scientific name: *Tachycineta bicolor*
Habitat: Fields
Diet: Insects
Nest site: In holes in trees and in bird boxes
Migration: Short distance and long distance
Location: NW NE SW SE

A Tree Swallow's chicks snuggle in their soft and feathery nest.

An adult Tree Swallow stuffs an insect into the mouth of one of its young. This family is using a bird box as a home.

A Tree Swallow in its woodpecker-made home.

Nature Note

Many of our swallows are named for where they nest:

- Barn Swallows often build mud nests in barns.
- Cliff Swallows often build mud nests under cliff ledges.
- Cave Swallows often build mud nests inside caves.
- Bank Swallows dig hole nests in riverbanks and eroded sandbanks.

Golden-crowned Kinglet

Kinglets

Tiny Winter Wonder

Golden-crowned Kinglets often hunt at the tips of branches in search of tiny moth caterpillars.

Size matters when you live in a cold environment. The larger you are, the easier it is for you to conserve heat, so many northern animals are bigger than their southern cousins. But the Golden-crowned Kinglet is *tiny* — half the weight of a Black-capped Chickadee. And these kinglets can survive temperatures as low as –30°F (–34°C) in their northern forest homes. How do they do it? It all has to do with food and insulation. Golden-crowned Kinglets feed on tiny moth caterpillars that overwinter on the tips of branches. They need to eat enough caterpillars every day to survive each cold night. At night, they fluff up their feathers to trap air, which helps keep their body heat in and the cold outside air out. Downy feathers are great at stopping heat loss, which is why down coats are so warm for us humans. Golden-crowned Kinglet feathers are so dense that they make up 8 percent of the bird's entire body weight. The kinglets also stay warm by cuddling together on the same branch while they are sleeping.

Life Size
3¾ inches
(9.5 cm)

This male Golden-crowned Kinglet shows off his orange crown while singing.

Nature Note

Golden-crowned Kinglets are the second-smallest bird species in North America, after hummingbirds.

Golden-crowned Kinglets are often found in forests with lots of conifers.

Adult Golden-crowned Kinglets have yellow crowns on the tops of their heads. The male also has orange feathers in the center of the yellow ones.

Scientific name: *Regulus satrapa*
Habitat: Forests
Diet: Insects, spiders and some seeds
Nest site: On tree branches
Migration: Resident and short distance
Location: NW NE SW SE

Cedar Waxwing

Waxwings

A Berry Nice Dancer

Courtship feeding is a common behavior in birds. This is when a male brings its potential mate a food gift to help cement their pair bond. Cedar Waxwings make this interaction even more interesting by adding dance moves. First the male finds a berry, insect or even a flower petal. He carries his gift in his beak, lands beside the female and then hops toward her and offers her the prize. If she is interested, she takes the gift, hops off and looks away, then she looks back and hops back toward the male. She then returns the gift to the male, who then hops away, and then they repeat the whole dance. The dance finishes when the female eats the prize. Scientists think that the male gives the female food to show her he will be able to provide food for their future nestlings.

Life Size
7 inches
(17.8 cm)

Scientific name: *Bombycilla cedrorum*
Habitat: Forests and fields with fruit trees
Diet: Fruit, flowers and insects
Nest site: On tree branches
Migration: Resident and short distance
Location: NW NE SW SE

A pair of Cedar Waxwings pass a berry back and forth to each other.

Outside of the breeding season, Cedar Waxwings are often found in large flocks.

Even Cedar Waxwing chicks love berries!

Nature Note

The Cedar Waxwing is a fruit specialist. It gets a meal and, in return, spreads the plant's seeds when it poops them out far from the parent plant — a natural partnership.

Mating may occur after the hopping dance.

Red-breasted Nuthatch

Nuthatches

The Upside-Down Bird

Up, down and sideways, the Red-breasted Nuthatch can move in any direction on the side of a tree trunk. This allows it to find insects and spiders hiding in cracks in the tree's bark. These critters may be missed by other tree-clinging birds, such as woodpeckers and creepers, which usually face upright. A nuthatch can move this way because of two great adaptations. It holds its legs closer to the middle of its body compared to most perching birds, which helps the nuthatch balance its body as it grips the vertical bark of a tree. And its great grip is a second adaptation. Nuthatches have extra-long claws on their strong back toes. These claws allow them to hold bark at various angles. They are especially important when the bird is facing downward.

Nature Note

Red-breasted Nuthatches are true tool users. They have been known to spread sticky sap at the entrances of their nest holes, possibly to stop mice and snakes from getting to their eggs and young.

Life Size
4¼ inches (11 cm)

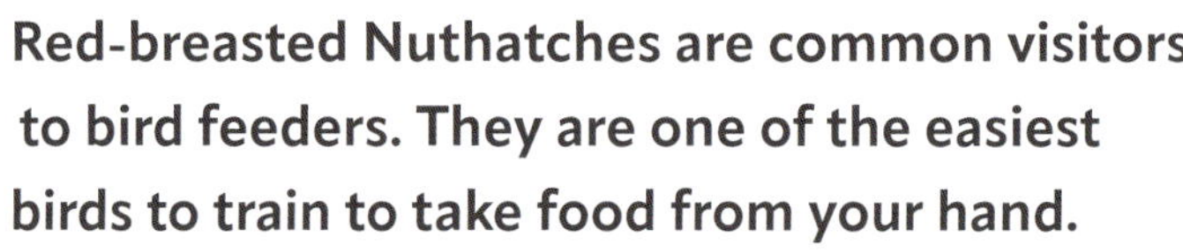

Red-breasted Nuthatches are common visitors to bird feeders. They are one of the easiest birds to train to take food from your hand.

Their sharp, wedge-shaped beaks help nuthatches search under bits of bark for hidden insects and probe conifer cones (including pine cones) for seeds. This White-breasted Nuthatch is about to wedge a seed into a crack so it can peck into it with its beak.

Note the long claw on the back toe (this toe is called the hallux) of this Red-breasted Nuthatch.

Scientific name: *Sitta canadensis*
Habitat: Forests
Diet: Insects and seeds
Nest site: In holes in trees
Migration: Resident and short distance
Location: NW NE SW SE

The other three nuthatches found in North America are the White-breasted Nuthatch, the Pygmy Nuthatch and the Brown-headed Nuthatch.

White-breasted Nuthatch

Pygmy Nuthatch

Brown-headed Nuthatch

Birding Is for Everyone!

Everyone in your family should try birdwatching, also called birding, to see if it is something they would enjoy. If you have decided to really get to know the birds in your area, there are some special tools that will make being a birder a lot easier. Binoculars are probably the most important piece of equipment. They help magnify the bird you are seeing, so you don't need to get too close and possibly disturb it. There are many different options for binoculars. The key is to get a pair that works best for you, so try different ones before you decide. A bird identification guide can also help you. Bird books can cover all of North America or just your state or province, so look around to see what is available and what works best for you. There are also field guide apps for cell phones. One great free app is called Merlin. It not only has photos and info on birds, it allows you to keep a list of what you see. The list of all the birds you have seen in your life is called a life list, and it is fun to see how many different species you can put on it. The platform eBird is another way to record your sightings, and it also allows scientists to use your data to study birds.

Using binoculars will make you happy!

Birding is an activity that the whole family can enjoy.

A notebook is an excellent way to record your sightings as well as sketch the birds you're seeing to help you remember what they look like.

Set goals for the birds you want to see. Not only will you have the thrill of eventually finding them, but you'll also get to explore new natural places along the way.

Some libraries have birding packages that include a pair of binoculars and a field guide that you can sign out and use in the field. Check to see if your local branch offers this service. Your family can also look up local naturalist groups. Many parks have regular birding hikes, which you can enjoy together. Most birders are happy to have beginners ask them questions, and they can tell you the best places to look for birds, too!

Birding Dos and Don'ts

When birding, remember these rules:

- **Don't get too close.** The bird's safety comes first. Try not to get too close to the bird. Birds will usually give you a signal that you are too close, so if they seem agitated, back away slowly.
- **Don't disturb bird nests.** Breeding birds and young birds are very vulnerable. Always be careful and keep your distance from birds' nests, eggs and young.
- **Do share birding with others.** Go out birdwatching with your family and friends. You never know who might really like it!
- **Do think about how you can incorporate your interest in birds into your schoolwork.** Science fair projects, poetry and art assignments are just a few ways you can express your interest in birds.
- **Do join local naturalist clubs.** These are great organizations for learning more about the birds in your area.

Brown Creeper

Creepers

Did That Piece of Bark Just Move?

Blending into bark is a Brown Creeper's superpower.

While nuthatches can climb in any direction (see page 92), the Brown Creeper is a specialist at climbing upward. It starts at the bottom of a tree and circles the trunk as it climbs up bit by bit. It supports itself with its stiff, pointed tail feathers, just like woodpeckers do. Once it has looked over the bark to its satisfaction, it flies to the bottom of the next tree and starts climbing up again. If it finds a tasty insect or spider in a small crack in the bark, it uses its long, thin tweezer-like beak to pull it out. Spending your life out in the open on tree trunks can be dangerous for a tiny bird like a Brown Creeper, but they have evolved to have detailed feather patterns that help them blend right into tree bark.

Life Size
5 inches (12.5 cm)

Long claws and a stiff tail help creepers hold firmly onto tree trunks and branches.

Scientific name: *Certhia americana*
Habitat: Forests
Diet: Insects and spiders
Nest site: On tree trunks, under peeling bark
Migration: Resident and short distance
Location: NW NE SW SE

Nature Note

To stay warm in winter, Brown Creepers may pile together in an old woodpecker hole or crack in a tree. There are at least five Brown Creepers huddled together in this winter roost.

House Wren

Wrens

Small but Mighty

Scientific name: *Troglodytes aedon*
Habitat: Forests and forest edges
Diet: Insects and spiders
Nest site: In holes in trees and in bird boxes
Migration: Resident and short distance
Location: NW NE SW SE

The House Wren is one of the smallest cavity-loving bird species. That means it likes to nest in holes. With its tiny size, you might think it would be at a disadvantage when it comes to getting a perfect tree cavity for its nest, but the House Wren is fierce. It has been known to destroy eggs and nestlings of competing cavity-nesting birds, such as woodpeckers, bluebirds, chickadees, Prothonotary Warblers and Tree Swallows. The male House Wren has another trick to help him control the cavities in his territory: dummy nests. He fills different cavities throughout his territory with sticks, sometimes right to the top. This stops other birds from using the cavity for their own nests. Scientists don't really know why the male House Wren does this, but it likely provides a female House Wren with a variety of nest cavities from which she can choose. The other "dummy" nests may also fool predators into thinking that none of the nests in the area have eggs in them, so they give up searching the nests. These extra nests may also attract a second female to the male's territory, which could result in him being able to father more young in one season than if he had only one mate.

Life Size
4½ inches (11.4 cm)

A House Wren peeks out of its cavity nest, always alert for intruders and predators.

Four nestlings await the next food delivery from their parents.

Nature Note

House Wrens are one of the easiest bird species to attract to a backyard bird box. Building the box is a great family project, and there are many plans online for you to choose from!

Insects are a favorite food for House Wrens.

Male House Wrens proclaim their territories with lively singing.

American Goldfinch

Finches and Allies

Dietary Defense

American Goldfinches' feathers are less colorful in the winter.

Scientific name: *Spinus tristis*
Habitat: Forest edges, fields and gardens
Diet: Seeds
Nest site: On tree branches or shrubs
Migration: Resident and short distance
Location: NW NE SW SE

The Brown-headed Cowbird (see pages 106–107) is a nest parasite that lays its eggs in the nests of many small songbirds. However, American Goldfinches have two defenses that ensure cowbirds aren't usually a problem for them, and both have to do with food. First, American Goldfinches nest much later in the season than other songbirds. They likely do this because thistle seeds, their favorite food, are only ready to be eaten in late summer. Since Brown-headed Cowbirds lay their eggs when most songbirds are nesting, they rarely end up laying their eggs in an American Goldfinch nest. When a female Brown-headed Cowbird happens to parasitize an American Goldfinch nest, the finch's second defense comes into play. Most songbird nestlings need to eat insects. The protein from them helps with processes such as growing feathers. Even birds that usually eat seeds as adults still feed insects to their young. However, American Goldfinch nestlings are able to get the protein they need from the seeds their parents feed them. They do not bring any insects to the nest. This is a disaster for a Brown-headed Cowbird chick. The cowbird can usually only grow for a few days on a diet of just seeds, and it will eventually die without the extra protein from insects. Although the American Goldfinch's unique reproductive timing and diet didn't likely evolve as a defense against nest parasitism, it certainly ended up being a successful nesting strategy.

A male American Goldfinch eats its favorite food: thistle seeds.

Nature Note

The American Goldfinch enjoys another benefit by nesting later in the season: prime nesting material. The downy "parachutes" that are attached to thistles and other late-summer seeds make a very soft nest for the goldfinch's eggs and young.

Life Size
4¾ inches (12.2 cm)

♂ ♀

Snow Bunting

Longspurs and Snow Buntings

Northernmost Nester

As its name suggests, the Snow Bunting can handle the cold. It nests way up north on the Arctic's northern islands. This makes it one of the world's northernmost nesting songbirds. It builds its nest in rock crevices to help protect its eggs and chicks from predators. Unfortunately, it is much colder deep in the rocks than on the open plains of the tundra. To prevent her eggs and young chicks from freezing, a female Snow Bunting spends much of her time on her nest. Her mate helps by delivering most of mom's food right to the nest. The mother bunting also keeps her babies warm by lining her nest with fur and feathers from Arctic animals such as the Arctic Fox, Arctic Hare, Rock Ptarmigan and Snowy Owl. Most Snow Buntings migrate south for the winter and spend their time in weedy fields, in open farmland and along shorelines. Snow Buntings are able to store lots of fat. This can be important for survival, especially for male buntings, who arrive at their Arctic nesting territories early in the spring, a month before the females.

Nature Note

While searching for food in their winter flocks, Snow Buntings often leapfrog over each other as they look for seeds across open fields covered in snow.

Hundreds of Snow Buntings may flock together on their wintering grounds in southern Canada and the northern United States.

This young Snow Bunting just left its protected nest site. It is almost ready to take on its Arctic life without its parents.

Life Size
6¾ inches (17.1 cm)

A male Snow Bunting in breeding plumage surveys his tundra nesting grounds.

Scientific name: *Plectrophenax nivalis*
Habitat: Open fields and tundra
Diet: Seeds, grains and insects
Nest site: In rock crevices
Migration: Resident and short distance
Location: NW NE

Baltimore Oriole

New World Blackbirds

From Species to Subspecies and Back Again

Life Size
8½ inches
(21.6 cm)

♂

Nature Note

The Baltimore Oriole is very similar to its two closest relatives: the Bullock's Oriole of western North America (left) and the Black-backed Oriole of central Mexico (right).

The Baltimore Oriole's clear-whistled song and brilliant orange-and-black feathers make it a favorite backyard bird. Having its name associated with a Major League Baseball team probably helps its popularity, too! But in 1973 scientists decided that the Baltimore Oriole was a subspecies and not actually a full species. A species normally only mates with others of its own kind. In some areas of North America, the eastern Baltimore Oriole often breeds with a different species, the more western Bullock's Oriole. The two birds look different, but scientists determined they were not different enough to be considered separate species. They were merged together into a single species called the Northern Oriole, and the different-looking populations were considered subspecies. Then in 1995 new scientists discovered more information about the relationships between the two Northern Oriole populations, and it was decided that they were different enough to be considered separate species after all. So we now have the Baltimore Oriole back as its own species. This lumping (classifying two or more species together into one species) and splitting (classifying two or more subspecies as separate species) is a way that we humans try to understand how nature works. The Baltimore Oriole and the Bullock's Oriole had a common ancestor many, many years ago. Over time, different habitat conditions in different parts of North America caused this ancestor to start evolving into separate species. The natural world is a dynamic place. (For more information on the classification of birds, see pages 40–41.)

A Baltimore Oriole builds its bag-like nest.

Scientific name: *Icterus galbula*
Habitat: Forests
Diet: Insects, fruit and nectar
Nest site: On tree branches
Migration: Short distance and long distance
Location: NW NE SE

Life Size

♀

Brown-headed Cowbird

Blackbirds

A Different Parenting Style

The Brown-headed Cowbird is known as an "obligate brood parasite." This means that the female always lays her eggs in the nests of other birds. She never makes her own nest. You might think this is the easy way out of parenting: Just dump your eggs, and someone else does all the work raising your young. But it is a bit more complicated than that. Most small birds lay four or five eggs in their own nest. If they can nest twice in one breeding season, they will lay about 8 to 10 eggs. A female Brown-headed Cowbird usually lays only one egg in a nest she finds. That egg could be rejected by the owner of the nest. To make sure at least some of her young are raised to adulthood, she lays an egg a day — for 40 days. That's 40 eggs every breeding season! And she must find a new nest for each egg. She may not have to raise her own young, but this bird's breeding strategy is not easy.

Life Size
7 inches (18 cm)

♂

Scientific name: *Molothrus ater*
Habitat: Fields and forest edges
Diet: Insects and seeds
Nest site: Uses other birds' nests
Migration: Resident and short distance
Location: NW NE SW SE

This Indigo Bunting nest has two of its own white eggs and one speckled Brown-headed Cowbird egg in it.

A Chipping Sparrow feeds its huge Brown-headed Cowbird chick at a bird feeder.

Nature Note

If you ever see a small bird feeding a young bird that is way bigger than itself, chances are that bird is an adoptive parent caring for a Brown-headed Cowbird chick.

Life Size

Northern Cardinal

Cardinals and Allies

Sing for Your Supper

The male Northern Cardinal's red plumage and crest make it one of our most recognizable backyard birds. His song is also a common sound of spring and summer, but female Northern Cardinals can sing, too. In North America, most female birds either don't sing or rarely sing, making the female Northern Cardinal's voice even more impressive. How she uses her song is also special. Although most small birds sing to claim a territory or find a mate, female Northern Cardinals often sing while sitting on their nest. When scientists studied a population of cardinals in Wisconsin, they found that when a male Northern Cardinal is ready to bring food to his mate at the nest, he sings to her from a distance. If she responds with a song that is different from his, it seems to mean she wants him to bring the food to the nest. If she sings a song that is similar to his song, it means she does not want him to come to the nest. These conversations happen at a distance, so they may help reduce the number of times the bright red male has to go to the nest. This makes it less likely that a predator sees where the nest is located.

The hidden nest of a Northern Cardinal.

A male Northern Cardinal waits to hear from his mate before bringing a meal to the nest.

Scientific name: *Cardinalis cardinalis*
Habitat: Forests, forest edges, shrubby areas, deserts and suburbs
Diet: Seeds, fruits, insects and spiders
Nest site: On shrubs or tangled vines
Migration: Resident
Location: NE SW SE

A female Northern Cardinal sings in the spring sunshine.

Nature Note

Northern Cardinals are the most popular official state birds in the United States. Seven states have chosen them as their favorite feathered friend, beating out the Western Meadowlark (six states) and the Northern Mockingbird (five states).

♀ ♂

Life Size
8¾ inches
(22.1 cm)

Index

Page numbers in *italics* mean charts and photos.